Dandelion Readers
from
Phonic Books Ltd

Handwriting sheets.

These sheets are to help with correct letter formation, which is so important in the early stages of writing. The order of the letters is linked to our books.

Letters are first presented on their own and then in 3 decreasing sizes and finally within words.

It is important to ask the child to say the sound as he/she writes the letter. This will help develop sound/symbol correspondence.

Should the school use a different letter shape in their handwriting scheme for some letters, then we would suggest making their own worksheets for those particular letters.

Contents

Unit 1 -   pages 1 to 14   a, i, m, s, t
Unit 2 -   pages 1 to 10   n, o, p
Unit 3 -   pages 1 to 14   b, c, g, h
Unit 4 -   pages 1 to 11   d, e, f, v
Unit 5 -   pages 1 to 10   k, l, r, u
Unit 6 -   pages 1 to 9   j, w, z
Unit 7 -   pages 1 to 7   x, y
Unit 16 - pages 1 to 4   q

Name: Date: Unit 1 page 1

Handwriting

Right handers slant their paper towards the left, left handers slant their paper towards the right. Ask child to write over the letter using as many different colours as possible, using coloured pencils, crayons or felt tips, saying the sound as he/she does it, to help acquire correct letter formation, and sound symbol correspondence. Dandelion Readers © 2007 This sheet may be photocopied by purchaser.

Name: Date: Unit 1 page 2

Handwriting

Right handers slant their paper towards the left, left handers slant their paper towards the right.
Ask child to go over the letter using as many different colours as possible, using coloured pencils, crayons or felt tips, to help acquire correct letter formation.
Dandelion Readers © 2007 This sheet may be photocopied by purchaser.

Name: Date: Unit 1 page 3

Handwriting

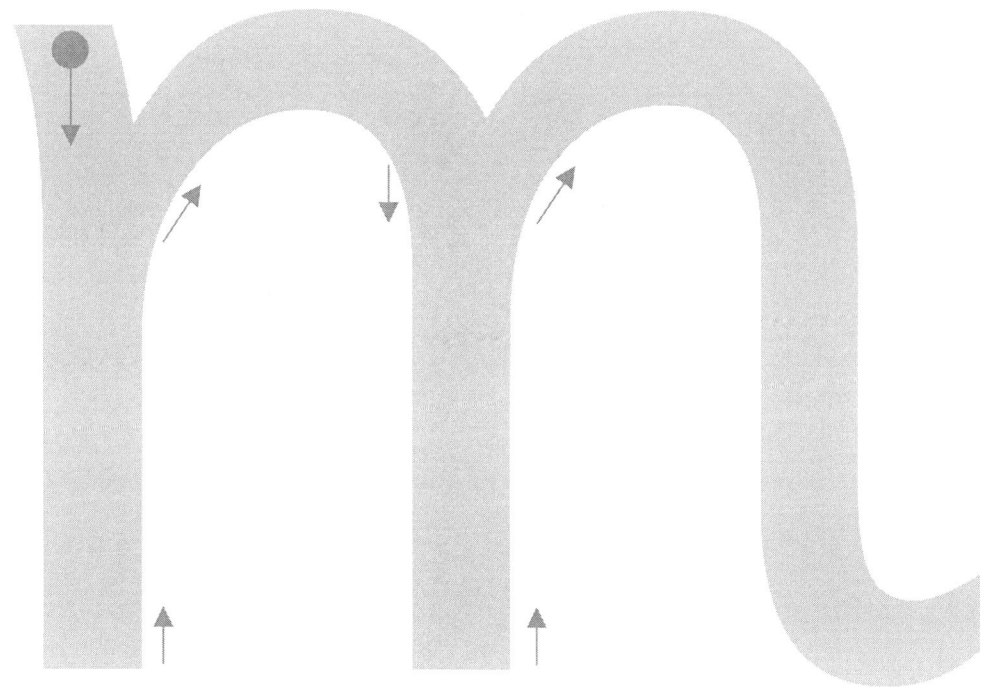

Right handers slant their paper towards the left, left handers slant their paper towards the right.
Ask child to go over the letter using as many different colours as possible, using coloured pencils, crayons or felt tips, to help acquire correct letter formation.
Dandelion Readers © 2007 This sheet may be photocopied by purchaser.

Name: Date: Unit 1 page 4

Handwriting

Right handers slant their paper towards the left, left handers slant their paper towards the right.
Ask child to go over the letter using as many different colours as possible, using coloured pencils,
crayons or felt tips, to help acquire correct letter formation.
Dandelion Readers © 2007 This sheet may be photocopied by purchaser.

Name: Date: Unit 1 page 5

Handwriting

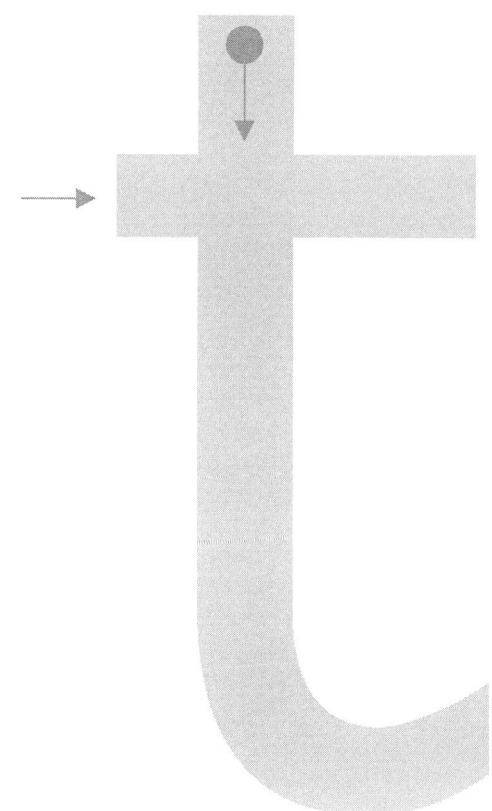

Right handers slant their paper towards the left, left handers slant their paper towards the right.
Ask child to go over the letter using as many different colours as possible, using coloured pencils, crayons or felt tips, to help acquire correct letter formation.
Dandelion Readers © 2007 This sheet may be photocopied by purchaser.

Name: Date: Unit 1 Page 6

Handwriting

a a a

a a a

a a a

Practise letter formation in the air, in wet sand, on sandpaper letters before writing them on paper.
Ask child to put a spot on where to start the letter for the whole line before beginning to write.
Doing this will help the child to focus on where to start writing.
Right handers slant their paper towards the left, left handers slant their paper towards the right.
The arrow points to where to start.
Ask child to whisper the sound as he/she writes it.
Do one sound a day for writing with young children.
Dandelion Readers © 2007 This sheet may be photocopied by the purchaser.

Name: Date: Unit 1 Page 7

Handwriting

i i i i i

i i i i i

i i i i i

Practise letter formation in the air, in wet sand, on sandpaper letters before writing them on paper.
Ask child to put a spot on where to start the letter for the whole line before beginning to write.
Doing this will help the child to focus on where to start writing.
Right handers slant their paper towards the left, left handers slant their paper towards the right.
The arrow points to where to start.
Ask child to whisper the sound as he/she writes it.
Do one sound a day for writing with young children.
Dandelion Readers © 2007 This sheet may be photocopied by the purchaser.

Name: Date: Unit 1 Page 8

Handwriting

↓• m m m

m m m

m m m

Practise letter formation in the air, in wet sand, on sandpaper letters before writing them on paper.
Ask child to put a spot on where to start the letter for the whole line before beginning to write.
Doing this will help the child to focus on where to start writing.
Right handers slant their paper towards the left, left handers slant their paper towards the right.
The arrow points to where to start.
Ask child to whisper the sound as he/she writes it.
Do one sound a day for writing with young children.
Dandelion Readers © 2007 This sheet may be photocopied by the purchaser.

Name: Date: Unit 1 Page 9

Handwriting

s s s s

s s s s

s s s s

Practise letter formation in the air, in wet sand, on sandpaper letters before writing them on paper.
Ask child to put a spot on where to start the letter for the whole line before beginning to write.
Doing this will help the child to focus on where to start writing.
Right handers slant their paper towards the left, left handers slant their paper towards the right.
The arrow points to where to start.
Ask child to whisper the sound as he/she writes it.
Do one sound a day for writing with young children.
Dandelion Readers © 2007 This sheet may be photocopied by the purchaser.

Name: Date: Unit 1 Page 10

Handwriting

t t t t

t t t t

t t t t

Practise letter formation in the air, in wet sand, on sandpaper letters before writing them on paper.
Ask child to put a spot on where to start the letter for the whole line before beginning to write.
Doing this will help the child to focus on where to start writing.
Right handers slant their paper towards the left, left handers slant their paper towards the right.
The arrow points to where to start.
Ask child to whisper the sound as he/she writes it.
Do one sound a day for writing with young children.
Dandelion Readers © 2007 This sheet may be photocopied by the purchaser.

Name: Date: Unit 1 Page 11

Handwriting

am am

am am

am am

Practise letter formation in the air, in wet sand, on sandpaper letters before writing them on paper.
Ask child to put a spot on where to start the letter for the whole line before beginning to write.
Doing this will help the child to focus on where to start writing.
Right handers slant their paper towards the left, left handers slant their paper towards the right.
The arrow points to where to start.
Ask child to whisper the sound as he/she writes it.
Do one sound a day for writing with young children.
Dandelion Readers © 2007 This sheet may be photocopied by the purchaser.

Name: Date: Unit 1 Page 12

Handwriting

is is is

it it it

at at at

Practise letter formation in the air, in wet sand, on sandpaper letters before writing them on paper.
Ask child to put a spot on where to start the letter for the whole line before beginning to write.
Doing this will help the child to focus on where to start writing.
Right handers slant their paper towards the left, left handers slant their paper towards the right.
The arrow points to where to start.
Ask child to whisper the sound as he/she writes it.
Do one sound a day for writing with young children.
Dandelion Readers © 2007 This sheet may be photocopied by the purchaser.

Name: Date: Unit 1 Page 13

Handwriting

a a a a a

i i i i i i i

t t t t t t

m m m m m

s s s s s s

Practise letter formation in the air, in wet sand, on sandpaper letters before writing them on paper.
The arrow points to where to start.
Right handers slant their paper towards the left, left handers slant their paper towards the right.
Ask child to whisper the sound as he/she writes it.
Do one sound a day for writing with young children.
Dandelion Readers © 2007 This sheet may be photocopied by the purchaser.

Name: Date   Unit 1 page 14

Handwriting

am am am am am

Sam Sam Sam Sam

it it it it it it it it

sit sit sit sit sit sit

Child can progress on to this sheet once he/she can form the letters correctly.
Right handers slant their paper towards the left, left handers slant their paper towards the right.
Ask child to read the word and then write over the letters saying the sounds as he/she writes.
Ask the child to write the same word on the line below saying the sounds as he/she writes.
Dandelion Readers © 2007 This sheet may be photocopied by the purchaser.

Name: Date: Unit 2 page 1

Handwriting

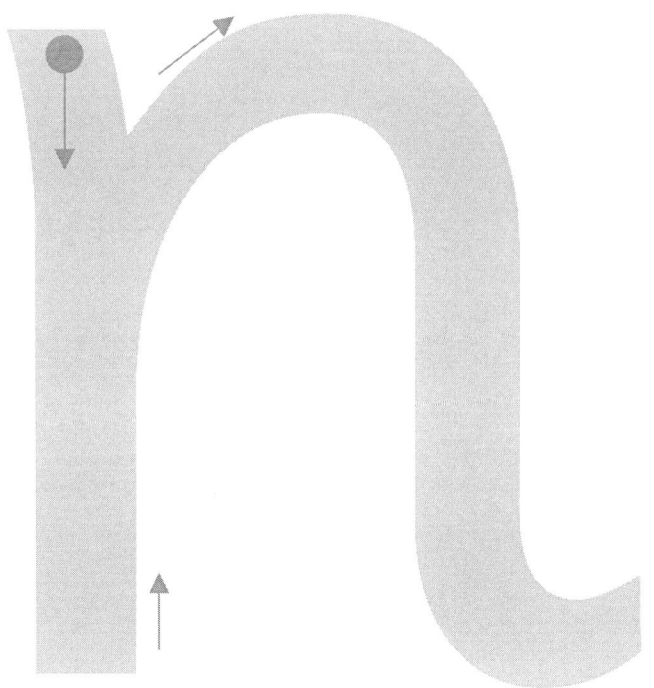

Right handers slant their paper towards the left, left handers slant their paper towards the right. Ask child to write over the letter using as many different colours as possible, using coloured pencils, crayons or felt tips, saying the sound as he/she does it, to help acquire correct letter formation, and sound symbol correspondence. Dandelion Readers © 2007 This sheet may be photocopied by purchaser.

Name: Date: Unit 2 page 2

Handwriting

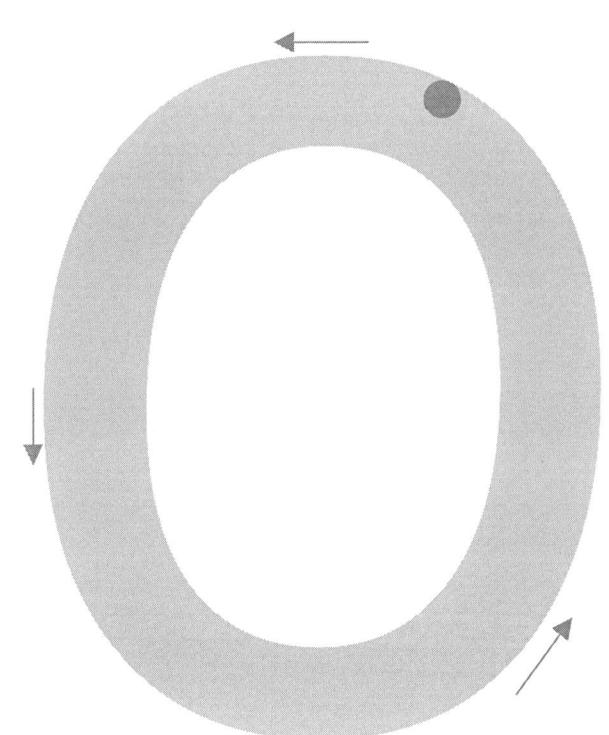

Right handers slant their paper towards the left, left handers slant their paper towards the right. Ask child to write over the letter using as many different colours as possible, using coloured pencils, crayons or felt tips, saying the sound as he/she does it, to help acquire correct letter formation, and sound symbol correspondence. Dandelion Readers © 2007 This sheet may be photocopied by purchaser.

Name: Date: Unit 2 page 3

Handwriting

Right handers slant their paper towards the left, left handers slant their paper towards the right.
Ask child to write over the letter using as many different colours as possible, using coloured pencils, crayons or
felt tips, saying the sound as he/she does it, to help acquire correct letter formation, and sound symbol
correspondence. Dandelion Readers © 2007 This sheet may be photocopied by purchaser.

Name: Date: Unit 2 Page 4

Handwriting

n n n n

n n n n

n n n n

Practise letter formation in the air, in wet sand, on sandpaper letters before writing them on paper.
Ask child to put a spot on where to start the letter for the whole line before beginning to write.
Doing this will help the child to focus on where to start writing.
Right handers slant their paper towards the left, left handers slant their paper towards the right.
The arrow points to where to start.
Ask child to whisper the sound as he/she writes it.
Do one sound a day for writing with young children.
Dandelion Readers © 2007 This sheet may be photocopied by the purchaser.

Name: Date: Unit 2 Page 5

Handwriting

Practise letter formation in the air, in wet sand, on sandpaper letters before writing them on paper.
Ask child to put a spot on where to start the letter for the whole line before beginning to write.
Doing this will help the child to focus on where to start writing.
Right handers slant their paper towards the left, left handers slant their paper towards the right.
The arrow points to where to start.
Ask child to whisper the sound as he/she writes it.
Do one sound a day for writing with young children.
Dandelion Readers © 2007 This sheet may be photocopied by the purchaser.

Name: Date: Unit 2 Page 6

Handwriting

p p p

p p p

p p p

Practise letter formation in the air, in wet sand, on sandpaper letters before writing them on paper.
Ask child to put a spot on where to start the letter for the whole line before beginning to write.
Doing this will help the child to focus on where to start writing.
Right handers slant their paper towards the left, left handers slant their paper towards the right.
The arrow points to where to start.
Ask child to whisper the sound as he/she writes it.
Do one sound a day for writing with young children.
Dandelion Readers © 2007 This sheet may be photocopied by the purchaser.

Name: Date: Unit 2 Page 7

Handwriting

on on

on on

on on

Practise letter formation in the air, in wet sand, on sandpaper letters before writing them on paper.
Ask child to put a spot on where to start the letter for the whole line before beginning to write.
Doing this will help the child to focus on where to start writing.
Right handers slant their paper towards the left, left handers slant their paper towards the right.
The arrow points to where to start.
Ask child to whisper the sound as he/she writes it.
Do one sound a day for writing with young children.
Dandelion Readers © 2007 This sheet may be photocopied by the purchaser.

Name: Date: Unit 2 Page 8

Handwriting

pip pip

pip pip

pip pip

Practise letter formation in the air, in wet sand, on sandpaper letters before writing them on paper.
Ask child to put a spot on where to start the letter for the whole line before beginning to write.
Doing this will help the child to focus on where to start writing.
Right handers slant their paper towards the left, left handers slant their paper towards the right.
The arrow points to where to start.
Ask child to whisper the sound as he/she writes it.
Do one sound a day for writing with young children.
Dandelion Readers © 2007 This sheet may be photocopied by the purchaser.

Name: Date: Unit 2 Page 9

Handwriting

n n n n n

o o o o o

p p p p p p

on on on on

pip pip pip

not not not

Practise letter formation in the air, in wet sand, on sandpaper letters before writing them on paper.
The arrow points to where to start.
Right handers slant their paper towards the left, left handers slant their paper towards the right.
Ask child to whisper the sound as he/she writes it.
Do one sound a day for writing with young children.
Dandelion Readers © 2007 This sheet may be photocopied by the purchaser.

Name: Date   Unit2 page 10

Handwriting

on   on   on   on   on   on

Pip   Pip   Pip   Pip   Pip

---

not   not   not   not   not

---

mop   mop   mop   mop

Child can progress on to this sheet once he/she can form the letters correctly.
Right handers slant their paper towards the left, left handers slant their paper towards the right.
Ask child to read the word and then write over the letters saying the sounds as he/she writes.
Ask the child to write the same word on the line below saying the sounds as he/she writes.
Dandelion Readers © 2007   This sheet may be photocopied by the purchaser.

Name: Date: Unit 3 page 1

Handwriting

Right handers slant their paper towards the left, left handers slant their paper towards the right. Ask child to write over the letter using as many different colours as possible, using coloured pencils, crayons or felt tips, saying the sound as he/she does it, to help acquire correct letter formation, and sound symbol correspondence. Dandelion Readers © 2007 This sheet may be photocopied by purchaser.

Name: Date: Unit 3 page 2

Handwriting

Right handers slant their paper towards the left, left handers slant their paper towards the right. Ask child to write over the letter using as many different colours as possible, using coloured pencils, crayons or felt tips, saying the sound as he/she does it, to help acquire correct letter formation, and sound symbol correspondence. Dandelion Readers © 2007 This sheet may be photocopied by purchaser.

Name: Date: Unit 3 page 3

Handwriting

Right handers slant their paper towards the left, left handers slant their paper towards the right. Ask child to write over the letter using as many different colours as possible, using coloured pencils, crayons or felt tips, saying the sound as he/she does it, to help acquire correct letter formation, and sound symbol correspondence. Dandelion Readers © 2007 This sheet may be photocopied by purchaser.

Name: Date: Unit 3 page 4

Handwriting

Right handers slant their paper towards the left, left handers slant their paper towards the right.
Ask child to write over the letter using as many different colours as possible, using coloured pencils, crayons or felt tips, saying the sound as he/she does it, to help acquire correct letter formation, and sound symbol correspondence. Dandelion Readers © 2007 This sheet may be photocopied by purchaser.

Name: Date: Unit 3 Page 5

Handwriting

b b b

b b b

b b b

Practise letter formation in the air, in wet sand, on sandpaper letters before writing them on paper.
Ask child to put a spot on where to start the letter for the whole line before beginning to write.
Doing this will help the child to focus on where to start writing.
Right handers slant their paper towards the left, left handers slant their paper towards the right.
The arrow points to where to start.
Ask child to whisper the sound as he/she writes it.
Do one sound a day for writing with young children.
Dandelion Readers © 2007 This sheet may be photocopied by the purchaser.

Name: Date: Unit 3 Page 6

Handwriting

c c c

c c c

c c c

Practise letter formation in the air, in wet sand, on sandpaper letters before writing them on paper.
Ask child to put a spot on where to start the letter for the whole line before beginning to write.
Doing this will help the child to focus on where to start writing.
Right handers slant their paper towards the left, left handers slant their paper towards the right.
The arrow points to where to start.
Ask child to whisper the sound as he/she writes it.
Do one sound a day for writing with young children.
Dandelion Readers © 2007 This sheet may be photocopied by the purchaser.

Name: Date: Unit 3 Page 7

Handwriting

Practise letter formation in the air, in wet sand, on sandpaper letters before writing them on paper.
Ask child to put a spot on where to start the letter for the whole line before beginning to write.
Doing this will help the child to focus on where to start writing.
Right handers slant their paper towards the left, left handers slant their paper towards the right.
The arrow points to where to start.
Ask child to whisper the sound as he/she writes it.
Do one sound a day for writing with young children.
Dandelion Readers © 2007 This sheet may be photocopied by the purchaser.

Name: Date: Unit 3 Page 8

Handwriting

Practise letter formation in the air, in wet sand, on sandpaper letters before writing them on paper.
Ask child to put a spot on where to start the letter for the whole line before beginning to write.
Doing this will help the child to focus on where to start writing.
Right handers slant their paper towards the left, left handers slant their paper towards the right.
The arrow points to where to start.
Ask child to whisper the sound as he/she writes it.
Do one sound a day for writing with young children.
Dandelion Readers © 2007 This sheet may be photocopied by the purchaser.

Name: Date: Unit 3 Page 9

Handwriting

bat bat

bin bin

sob sob

Practise letter formation in the air, in wet sand, on sandpaper letters before writing them on paper.
Ask child to put a spot on where to start the letter for the whole line before beginning to write.
Doing this will help the child to focus on where to start writing.
Right handers slant their paper towards the left, left handers slant their paper towards the right.
The arrow points to where to start.
Ask child to whisper the sound as he/she writes it.
Do one sound a day for writing with young children.
Dandelion Readers © 2007 This sheet may be photocopied by the purchaser.

Name: Date: Unit 3 Page 10

Handwriting

cat   cat

cab   cab

cot   cot

Practise letter formation in the air, in wet sand, on sandpaper letters before writing them on paper.
Ask child to put a spot on where to start the letter for the whole line before beginning to write.
Doing this will help the child to focus on where to start writing.
Right handers slant their paper towards the left, left handers slant their paper towards the right.
The arrow points to where to start.
Ask child to whisper the sound as he/she writes it.
Do one sound a day for writing with young children.
Dandelion Readers © 2007 This sheet may be photocopied by the purchaser.

Name: Date: Unit 3 Page 11

Handwriting

gas gas

big big

got got

Practise letter formation in the air, in wet sand, on sandpaper letters before writing them on paper.
Ask child to put a spot on where to start the letter for the whole line before beginning to write.
Doing this will help the child to focus on where to start writing.
Right handers slant their paper towards the left, left handers slant their paper towards the right.
The arrow points to where to start.
Ask child to whisper the sound as he/she writes it.
Do one sound a day for writing with young children.
Dandelion Readers © 2007 This sheet may be photocopied by the purchaser.

Name: Date: Unit 3 Page 12

Handwriting

hat hat

him him

hop hop

Practise letter formation in the air, in wet sand, on sandpaper letters before writing them on paper.
Ask child to put a spot on where to start the letter for the whole line before beginning to write.
Doing this will help the child to focus on where to start writing.
Right handers slant their paper towards the left, left handers slant their paper towards the right.
The arrow points to where to start.
Ask child to whisper the sound as he/she writes it.
Do one sound a day for writing with young children.
Dandelion Readers © 2007 This sheet may be photocopied by the purchaser.

Name: Date: Unit 3 Page 13

Handwriting

b b b b b

c c c c c c

g g g g g g

h h h h h h

bag hob cot

Practise letter formation in the air, in wet sand, on sandpaper letters before writing them on paper.
The arrow points to where to start.
Right handers slant their paper towards the left, left handers slant their paper towards the right.
Ask child to whisper the sound as he/she writes it.
Do one sound a day for writing with young children.
Dandelion Readers © 2007 This sheet may be photocopied by the purchaser.

Name: Date Unit 3 page 14

Handwriting

bag bag bag bag

___

cab cab cab cab

___

him him him him

___

got got got got got

___

Child can progress on to this sheet once he/she can form the letters correctly.
Right handers slant their paper towards the left, left handers slant their paper towards the right.
Ask child to read the word and then write over the letters saying the sounds as he/she writes.
Ask the child to write the same word on the line below saying the sounds as he/she writes.
Dandelion Readers © 2007 This sheet may be photocopied by the purchaser.

Name: Date: Unit 4 page 1

Handwriting

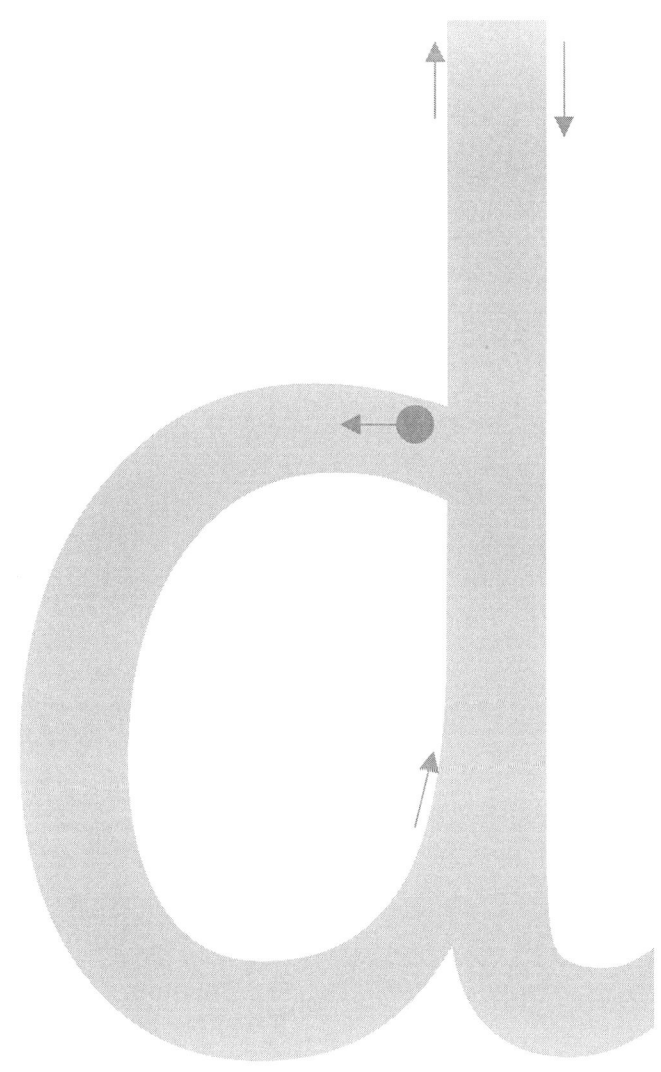

Right handers slant their paper towards the left, left handers slant their paper towards the right. Ask child to write over the letter using as many different colours as possible, using coloured pencils, crayons or felt tips, saying the sound as he/she does it, to help acquire correct letter formation, and sound symbol correspondence. Dandelion Readers © 2007 This sheet may be photocopied by purchaser.

Name: Date: Unit 4 page 2

Handwriting

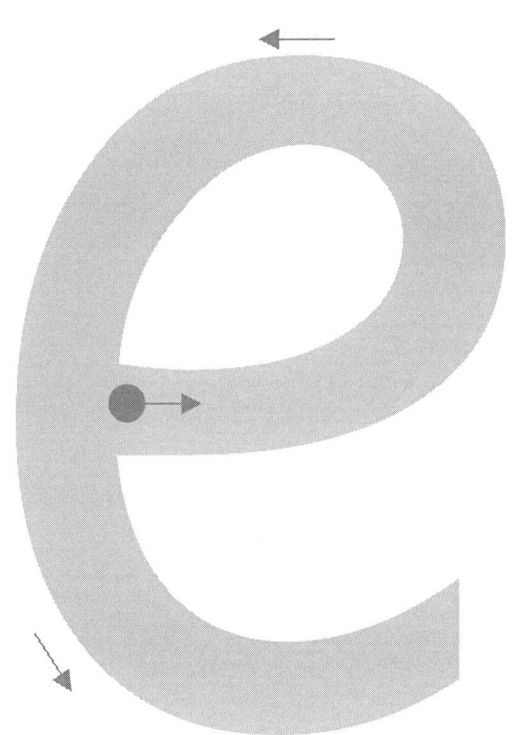

Right handers slant their paper towards the left, left handers slant their paper towards the right. Ask child to write over the letter using as many different colours as possible, using coloured pencils, crayons or felt tips, saying the sound as he/she does it, to help acquire correct letter formation, and sound symbol correspondence. Dandelion Readers © 2007 This sheet may be photocopied by purchaser.

Name: Date: Unit 4 page 3

Handwriting

Right handers slant their paper towards the left, left handers slant their paper towards the right. Ask child to write over the letter using as many different colours as possible, using coloured pencils, crayons or felt tips, saying the sound as he/she does it, to help acquire correct letter formation, and sound symbol correspondence. Dandelion Readers © 2007 This sheet may be photocopied by purchaser.

| Name: | Date: | Unit 4 page 4 |

Handwriting

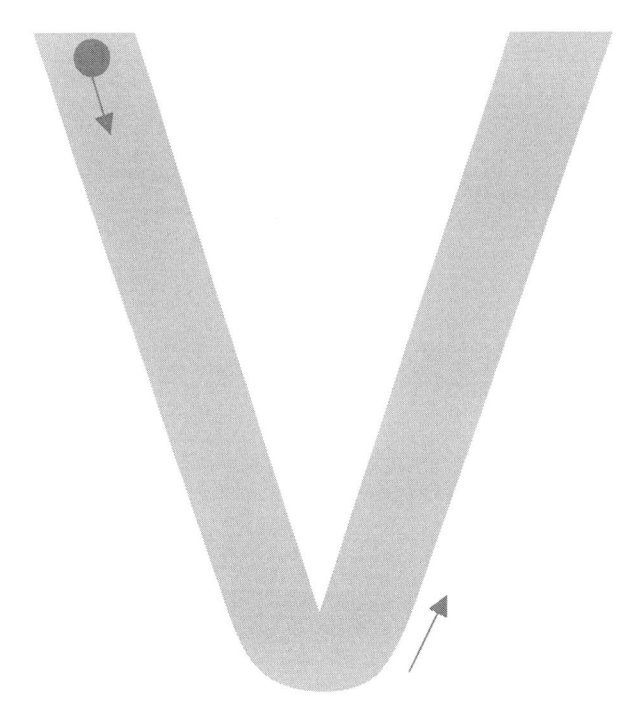

Right handers slant their paper towards the left, left handers slant their paper towards the right. Ask child to write over the letter using as many different colours as possible, using coloured pencils, crayons or felt tips, saying the sound as he/she does it, to help acquire correct letter formation, and sound symbol correspondence. Dandelion Readers © 2007 This sheet may be photocopied by purchaser.

Name: Date: Unit 4 Page 5

Handwriting

d d d

d d d

d d d

Practise letter formation in the air, in wet sand, on sandpaper letters before writing them on paper.
Ask child to put a spot on where to start the letter for the whole line before beginning to write.
Doing this will help the child to focus on where to start writing.
Right handers slant their paper towards the left, left handers slant their paper towards the right.
The arrow points to where to start.
Ask child to whisper the sound as he/she writes it.
Do one sound a day for writing with young children.
Dandelion Readers © 2007 This sheet may be photocopied by the purchaser.

Name: Date: Unit 4 Page 6

Handwriting

e e e

e e e

e e e

Practise letter formation in the air, in wet sand, on sandpaper letters before writing them on paper.
Ask child to put a spot on where to start the letter for the whole line before beginning to write.
Doing this will help the child to focus on where to start writing.
Right handers slant their paper towards the left, left handers slant their paper towards the right.
The arrow points to where to start.
Ask child to whisper the sound as he/she writes it.
Do one sound a day for writing with young children.
Dandelion Readers © 2007 This sheet may be photocopied by the purchaser.

Name: Date: Unit 4 Page 7

Handwriting

f f f

f f f f

f f f f

Practise letter formation in the air, in wet sand, on sandpaper letters before writing them on paper.
Ask child to put a spot on where to start the letter for the whole line before beginning to write.
Doing this will help the child to focus on where to start writing.
Right handers slant their paper towards the left, left handers slant their paper towards the right.
The arrow points to where to start.
Ask child to whisper the sound as he/she writes it.
Do one sound a day for writing with young children.
Dandelion Readers © 2007 This sheet may be photocopied by the purchaser.

Name: Date: Unit 4 Page 8

Handwriting

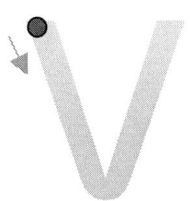  

Practise letter formation in the air, in wet sand, on sandpaper letters before writing them on paper.
Ask child to put a spot on where to start the letter for the whole line before beginning to write.
Doing this will help the child to focus on where to start writing.
Right handers slant their paper towards the left, left handers slant their paper towards the right.
The arrow points to where to start.
Ask child to whisper the sound as he/she writes it.
Do one sound a day for writing with young children.
Dandelion Readers © 2007 This sheet may be photocopied by the purchaser.

Name: Date: Unit 4 Page 9

Handwriting

fed fed

vet vet

bed bed

Practise letter formation in the air, in wet sand, on sandpaper letters before writing them on paper.
Ask child to put a spot on where to start the letter for the whole line before beginning to write.
Doing this will help the child to focus on where to start writing.
Right handers slant their paper towards the left, left handers slant their paper towards the right.
The arrow points to where to start.
Ask child to whisper the sound as he/she writes it.
Do one sound a day for writing with young children.
Dandelion Readers © 2007 This sheet may be photocopied by the purchaser.

Name: Date: Unit 4 Page 10

Handwriting

d d d d d

e e e e e e

f f f f f f f

v v v v v v v

fed vet bed

Practise letter formation in the air, in wet sand, on sandpaper letters before writing them on paper.
The arrow points to where to start.
Right handers slant their paper towards the left, left handers slant their paper towards the right.
Ask child to whisper the sound as he/she writes it.
Do one sound a day for writing with young children.
Dandelion Readers © 2007 This sheet may be photocopied by the purchaser.

Name: Date Unit 4 page 11

Handwriting

fed fed fed fed fed

vet vet vet vet vet

did did did did did

bed bed bed bed bed

Child can progress on to this sheet once he/she can form the letters correctly.
Right handers slant their paper towards the left, left handers slant their paper towards the right.
Ask child to read the word and then write over the letters saying the sounds as he/she writes.
Ask the child to write the same word on the line below saying the sounds as he/she writes.
Dandelion Readers © 2007 This sheet may be photocopied by the purchaser.

Name: Date: Unit 5 page 1

Handwriting

Right handers slant their paper towards the left, left handers slant their paper towards the right. Ask child to write over the letter using as many different colours as possible, using coloured pencils, crayons or felt tips, saying the sound as he/she does it, to help acquire correct letter formation, and sound symbol correspondence. Dandelion Readers © 2007 This sheet may be photocopied by purchaser.

Name: Date: Unit 5 page 2

Handwriting

Right handers slant their paper towards the left, left handers slant their paper towards the right. Ask child to write over the letter using as many different colours as possible, using coloured pencils, crayons or felt tips, saying the sound as he/she does it, to help acquire correct letter formation, and sound symbol correspondence. Dandelion Readers © 2007 This sheet may be photocopied by purchaser.

Name: Date: Unit 5 page 3

Handwriting

Right handers slant their paper towards the left, left handers slant their paper towards the right. Ask child to write over the letter using as many different colours as possible, using coloured pencils, crayons or felt tips, saying the sound as he/she does it, to help acquire correct letter formation, and sound symbol correspondence. Dandelion Readers © 2007 This sheet may be photocopied by purchaser.

Name: Date: Unit 5 page 4

Handwriting

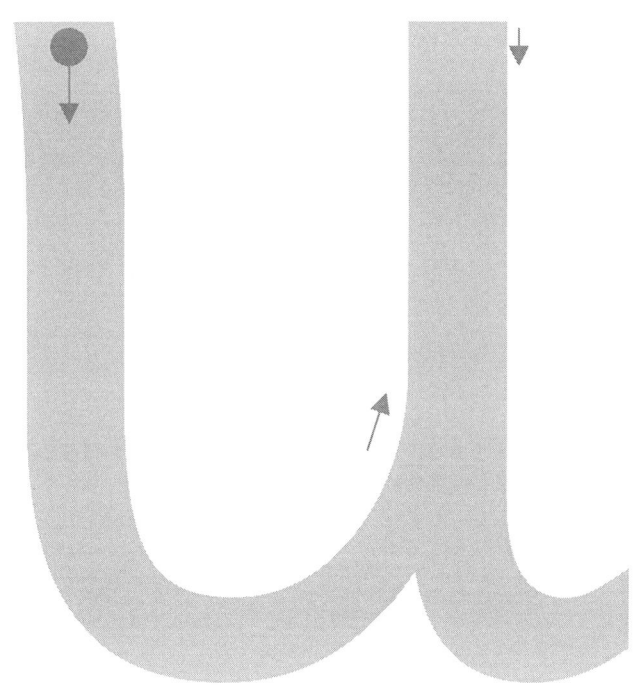

Right handers slant their paper towards the left, left handers slant their paper towards the right. Ask child to write over the letter using as many different colours as possible, using coloured pencils, crayons or felt tips, saying the sound as he/she does it, to help acquire correct letter formation, and sound symbol correspondence. Dandelion Readers © 2007 This sheet may be photocopied by purchaser.

Name: Date: Unit 5 Page 5

Handwriting

k k k

k k k

k k k

Practise letter formation in the air, in wet sand, on sandpaper letters before writing them on paper.
Ask child to put a spot on where to start the letter for the whole line before beginning to write.
Doing this will help the child to focus on where to start writing.
Right handers slant their paper towards the left, left handers slant their paper towards the right.
The arrow points to where to start.
Ask child to whisper the sound as he/she writes it.
Do one sound a day for writing with young children.
Dandelion Readers © 2007 This sheet may be photocopied by the purchaser.

Name: Date: Unit 5 Page 6

Handwriting

l l l l l

l l l l l

l l l l l

Practise letter formation in the air, in wet sand, on sandpaper letters before writing them on paper.
Ask child to put a spot on where to start the letter for the whole line before beginning to write.
Doing this will help the child to focus on where to start writing.
Right handers slant their paper towards the left, left handers slant their paper towards the right.
The arrow points to where to start.
Ask child to whisper the sound as he/she writes it.
Do one sound a day for writing with young children.
Dandelion Readers © 2007 This sheet may be photocopied by the purchaser.

Name: Date: Unit 5 Page 7

Handwriting

Practise letter formation in the air, in wet sand, on sandpaper letters before writing them on paper.
Ask child to put a spot on where to start the letter for the whole line before beginning to write.
Doing this will help the child to focus on where to start writing.
Right handers slant their paper towards the left, left handers slant their paper towards the right.
The arrow points to where to start.
Ask child to whisper the sound as he/she writes it.
Do one sound a day for writing with young children.
Dandelion Readers © 2007 This sheet may be photocopied by the purchaser.

Name: Date: Unit 5 Page 8

Handwriting

u u u

u u u

u u u

Practise letter formation in the air, in wet sand, on sandpaper letters before writing them on paper.
Ask child to put a spot on where to start the letter for the whole line before beginning to write.
Doing this will help the child to focus on where to start writing.
Right handers slant their paper towards the left, left handers slant their paper towards the right.
The arrow points to where to start.
Ask child to whisper the sound as he/she writes it.
Do one sound a day for writing with young children.
Dandelion Readers © 2007 This sheet may be photocopied by the purchaser.

Name: Date: Unit 5 Page 9

Handwriting

kid kid

rug rug

lad lad

Practise letter formation in the air, in wet sand, on sandpaper letters before writing them on paper.
Ask child to put a spot on where to start the letter for the whole line before beginning to write.
Doing this will help the child to focus on where to start writing.
Right handers slant their paper towards the left, left handers slant their paper towards the right.
The arrow points to where to start.
Ask child to whisper the sound as he/she writes it.
Do one sound a day for writing with young children.
Dandelion Readers © 2007 This sheet may be photocopied by the purchaser.

Name: Date: Unit 5 Page 10

Handwriting

k k k k k k

l l l l l l l

r r r r r r r

u u u u u u

kid rug lad

Practise letter formation in the air, in wet sand, on sandpaper letters before writing them on paper.
The arrow points to where to start.
Right handers slant their paper towards the left, left handers slant their paper towards the right.
Ask child to whisper the sound as he/she writes it.
Do one sound a day for writing with young children.
Dandelion Readers © 2007 This sheet may be photocopied by the purchaser.

Name: Date Unit 5 page 11

Handwriting

kid kid kid kid kid

rug rug rug rug rug

lad lad lad lad lad

bed bed bed bed bed

Child can progress on to this sheet once he/she can form the letters correctly.
Right handers slant their paper towards the left, left handers slant their paper towards the right.
Ask child to read the word and then write over the letters saying the sounds as he/she writes.
Ask the child to write the same word on the line below saying the sounds as he/she writes.
Dandelion Readers © 2007 This sheet may be photocopied by the purchaser.

Name: Date: Unit 6 page 1

Handwriting

Right handers slant their paper towards the left, left handers slant their paper towards the right. Ask child to write over the letter using as many different colours as possible, using coloured pencils, crayons or felt tips, saying the sound as he/she does it, to help acquire correct letter formation, and sound symbol correspondence. Dandelion Readers © 2007 This sheet may be photocopied by purchaser.

Name: Date: Unit 6 page 2

Handwriting

Right handers slant their paper towards the left, left handers slant their paper towards the right. Ask child to write over the letter using as many different colours as possible, using coloured pencils, crayons or felt tips, saying the sound as he/she does it, to help acquire correct letter formation, and sound symbol correspondence. Dandelion Readers © 2007 This sheet may be photocopied by purchaser.

Name: Date: Unit 6 page 3

Handwriting

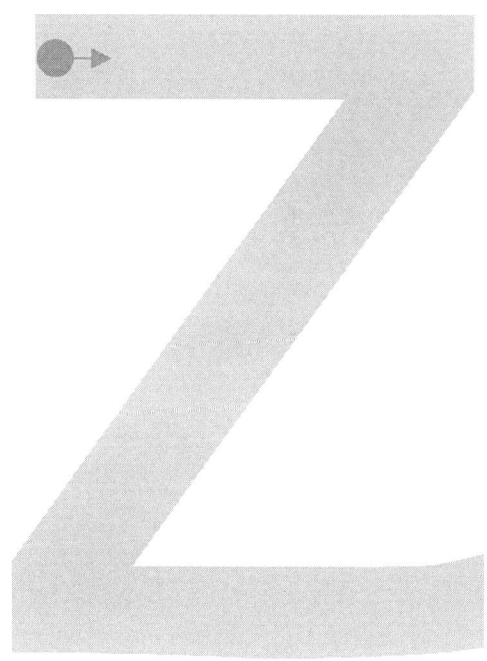

Right handers slant their paper towards the left, left handers slant their paper towards the right. Ask child to write over the letter using as many different colours as possible, using coloured pencils, crayons or felt tips, saying the sound as he/she does it, to help acquire correct letter formation, and sound symbol correspondence. Dandelion Readers © 2007 This sheet may be photocopied by purchaser.

Name: Date: Unit 6 Page 4

Handwriting

Practise letter formation in the air, in wet sand, on sandpaper letters before writing them on paper.
Ask child to put a spot on where to start the letter for the whole line before beginning to write.
Doing this will help the child to focus on where to start writing.
Right handers slant their paper towards the left, left handers slant their paper towards the right.
The arrow points to where to start.
Ask child to whisper the sound as he/she writes it.
Do one sound a day for writing with young children.
Dandelion Readers © 2007 This sheet may be photocopied by the purchaser.

Name: Date: Unit 6 Page 5

Handwriting

Practise letter formation in the air, in wet sand, on sandpaper letters before writing them on paper.
Ask child to put a spot on where to start the letter for the whole line before beginning to write.
Doing this will help the child to focus on where to start writing.
Right handers slant their paper towards the left, left handers slant their paper towards the right.
The arrow points to where to start.
Ask child to whisper the sound as he/she writes it.
Do one sound a day for writing with young children.
Dandelion Readers © 2007 This sheet may be photocopied by the purchaser.

Name: Date: Unit 6 Page 6

Handwriting

z z z z z

z z z z z

z z z z z

Practise letter formation in the air, in wet sand, on sandpaper letters before writing them on paper.
Ask child to put a spot on where to start the letter for the whole line before beginning to write.
Doing this will help the child to focus on where to start writing.
Right handers slant their paper towards the left, left handers slant their paper towards the right.
The arrow points to where to start.
Ask child to whisper the sound as he/she writes it.
Do one sound a day for writing with young children.
Dandelion Readers © 2007 This sheet may be photocopied by the purchaser.

Name: Date: Unit 6 Page 7

Handwriting

jam jam

wet wet

zip   zip

Practise letter formation in the air, in wet sand, on sandpaper letters before writing them on paper.
Ask child to put a spot on where to start the letter for the whole line before beginning to write.
Doing this will help the child to focus on where to start writing.
Right handers slant their paper towards the left, left handers slant their paper towards the right.
The arrow points to where to start.
Ask child to whisper the sound as he/she writes it.
Do one sound a day for writing with young children.
Dandelion Readers © 2007 This sheet may be photocopied by the purchaser.

Name: Date: Unit 6 Page 8

Handwriting

j j j j j j j j

w w w w w w w

z z z z z z z

jam   wet   zip

jam   wet   zip

Practise letter formation in the air, in wet sand, on sandpaper letters before writing them on paper.
The arrow points to where to start.
Right handers slant their paper towards the left, left handers slant their paper towards the right.
Ask child to whisper the sound as he/she writes it.
Do one sound a day for writing with young children.
Dandelion Readers © 2007 This sheet may be photocopied by the purchaser.

Name: Date   Unit 6 page 9

Handwriting

jet   jam   jet   jam   jet   jam

wet   win   wet   win   wet

zig   zag   zip   zig   zag   zip

jog   win   zip   jam   wet   zap

Child can progress on to this sheet once he/she can form the letters correctly.
Right handers slant their paper towards the left, left handers slant their paper towards the right.
Ask child to read the word and then write over the letters saying the sounds as he/she writes.
Ask the child to write the same word on the line below saying the sounds as he/she writes.
Dandelion Readers © 2007 This sheet may be photocopied by the purchaser.

Name: Date: Unit 7 page 1

Handwriting

Right handers slant their paper towards the left, left handers slant their paper towards the right. Ask child to write over the letter using as many different colours as possible, using coloured pencils, crayons or felt tips, saying the sound as he/she does it, to help acquire correct letter formation, and sound symbol correspondence. Dandelion Readers © 2007 This sheet may be photocopied by purchaser.

Name: Date: Unit 7 page 2

Handwriting

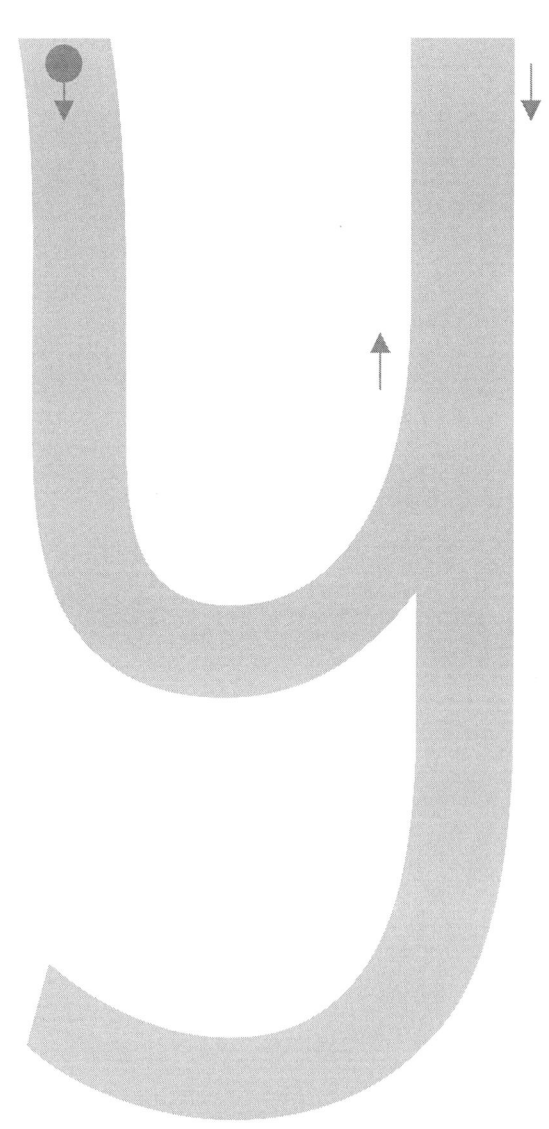

Right handers slant their paper towards the left, left handers slant their paper towards the right. Ask child to write over the letter using as many different colours as possible, using coloured pencils, crayons or felt tips, saying the sound as he/she does it, to help acquire correct letter formation, and sound symbol correspondence. Dandelion Readers © 2007 This sheet may be photocopied by purchaser.

Name: Date: Unit 7 Page 3

Handwriting

Practise letter formation in the air, in wet sand, on sandpaper letters before writing them on paper.
Ask child to put a spot on where to start the letter for the whole line before beginning to write.
Doing this will help the child to focus on where to start writing.
Right handers slant their paper towards the left, left handers slant their paper towards the right.
The arrow points to where to start.
Ask child to whisper the sound as he/she writes it.
Do one sound a day for writing with young children.
Dandelion Readers © 2007 This sheet may be photocopied by the purchaser.

Name: Date: Unit 7 Page 4

Handwriting

y y y y

y y y y

y y y y

Practise letter formation in the air, in wet sand, on sandpaper letters before writing them on paper.
Ask child to put a spot on where to start the letter for the whole line before beginning to write.
Doing this will help the child to focus on where to start writing.
Right handers slant their paper towards the left, left handers slant their paper towards the right.
The arrow points to where to start.
Ask child to whisper the sound as he/she writes it.
Do one sound a day for writing with young children.
Dandelion Readers © 2007 This sheet may be photocopied by the purchaser.

Name: Date: Unit 7 Page 5

Handwriting

box six

yet yes

yell mix

Practise letter formation in the air, in wet sand, on sandpaper letters before writing them on paper.
Ask child to put a spot on where to start the letter for the whole line before beginning to write.
Doing this will help the child to focus on where to start writing.
Right handers slant their paper towards the left, left handers slant their paper towards the right.
The arrow points to where to start.
Ask child to whisper the sound as he/she writes it.
Do one sound a day for writing with young children.
Dandelion Readers © 2007 This sheet may be photocopied by the purchaser.

Name: Date: Unit 7 Page 6

Handwriting

x x x x x x

y y y y y y

yes box yet six

fix yell mix yam

yak tax yob fox

Practise letter formation in the air, in wet sand, on sandpaper letters before writing them on paper.
The arrow points to where to start.
Right handers slant their paper towards the left, left handers slant their paper towards the right.
Ask child to whisper the sound as he/she writes it.
Do one sound a day for writing with young children.
Dandelion Readers © 2007 This sheet may be photocopied by the purchaser.

Name: Date Unit 7 page 7

Handwriting

box   six   fox   vex   mix

yes   yak   yet   yap   yam

box   six   fox   vex   mix

yes   yak   yet   yap   yam

Child can progress on to this sheet once he/she can form the letters correctly.
Right handers slant their paper towards the left, left handers slant their paper towards the right.
Ask child to read the word and then write over the letters saying the sounds as he/she writes.
Ask the child to write the same word on the line below saying the sounds as he/she writes.
Dandelion Readers © 2007 This sheet may be photocopied by the purchaser.

Name: Date: Unit 16 page 1

Handwriting

Right handers slant their paper towards the left, left handers slant their paper towards the right.
Ask child to write over the letter using as many different colours as possible, using coloured pencils, crayons or felt tips, saying the sound as he/she does it, to help acquire correct letter formation, and sound symbol correspondence. Dandelion Readers © 2007 This sheet may be photocopied by purchaser.

Name: Date: Unit 16 Page 2

Handwriting

Practise letter formation in the air, in wet sand, on sandpaper letters before writing them on paper.
Ask child to put a spot on where to start the letter for the whole line before beginning to write.
Doing this will help the child to focus on where to start writing.
Right handers slant their paper towards the left, left handers slant their paper towards the right.
The arrow points to where to start.
Ask child to whisper the sound as he/she writes it.
Do one sound a day for writing with young children.
Dandelion Readers © 2007 This sheet may be photocopied by the purchaser.

Name: Date: Unit 16 Page 3

Handwriting

q q q q q q

q q q q q q

quit quest quiz

quick quilt squid

quack quell quid

Practise letter formation in the air, in wet sand, on sandpaper letters before writing them on paper.
The arrow points to where to start.
Right handers slant their paper towards the left, left handers slant their paper towards the right.
Ask child to whisper the sound as he/she writes it.
Do one sound a day for writing with young children.
Dandelion Readers © 2007 This sheet may be photocopied by the purchaser.

Name:　　　　　　　　　Date　　　　　　　　　Unit 16　page 4

Handwriting

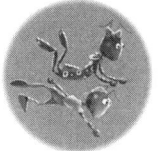

quit　quest　quilt　quack

---

quench　quill　quiz　quiff

---

quit　quest　quilt　quack

---

quench　quill　quiz　quiff

Child can progress on to this sheet once he/she can form the letters correctly.
Right handers slant their paper towards the left, left handers slant their paper towards the right.
Ask child to read the word and then write over the letters saying the sounds as he/she writes.
Ask the child to write the same word on the line below saying the sounds as he/she writes.
Dandelion Readers © 2007 This sheet may be photocopied by the purchaser.